twelve
FRAGMENTS
Thoughts for Today's Christian

By George Wilkie

SCOTTISH CHRISTIAN PRESS

First published in Great Britain
In 2005 by Scottish Christian Press
21 Young Street
Edinburgh EH2 4HU

Copyright © George Wilkie

All rights reserved. No part of this publication may be reproduced or transmitted in any form or by any means, electronic or mechanical, including photocopy, recording, or by any information storage or retrieval system, without written permission from the publisher.

George Wilkie has asserted his right under the Copyright, Designs and Patents Act 1988 to be identified as the author of this work.

ISBN 1904325335

Cover design and layout by Heather Macpherson
Typeset by Heather Macpherson

Printed and bound in the UK by Bookchase Ltd

In my youth I regarded the universe as an open book, printed in the language of physical equations and social determinants: whereas now it appears to me as a text written in invisible ink, of which in rare moments of grace, we are able to decipher a small fragment.

Arthur Koestler

CONTENTS

Introduction	1
Change	3
Mystery	5
Poetry	7
Ourselves	9
Religion	11
Creed	13
God	15
Church	17
Jesus	19
Cross	21
Faith(s)	23
Followers	25
References	27
Acknowledgements	30

INTRODUCTION

The impetus for setting down these 'fragments' came from a conversation I had with a long-serving elder of the Kirk. After rehearsing the various signs of decline in church life, he said: 'Although I still go to church, I find it difficult to repeat the Creed with any honesty or conviction. The world has moved on and these old statements of belief don't seem to fit in with what we know of the Universe and man's place in it.'

In recent months I have heard of a number of other long-standing elders who have resigned their membership of the church, or just stopped going, or who claim to be 'Christian Agnostics' or find huge obstacles in the traditional Statements of Faith for thinking men and women today.

As a minister of the church I've had to face these questions too. And I have to confess that there's a great deal of re-interpretation and de-mythologising going on as I strive to give some credibility to parts of these statements of belief.

Lay men and women tend not to be drawn into this process. In the name of shielding them from 'unnecessary anxieties', we ministers have left them thinking that 'real' Christians must accept a whole corpus of doctrine expressed in the language and thought-forms of a past age. There is an urgent need to draw such lay men and women into our thinking and in so doing discover with them a genuine faith that will stand up in the hostile climate of the 21st Century.

This is what I'm trying to do here, in a small way. A comprehensive statement is beyond me, so I've chosen to produce these fragments, or ideas, which deal with some of the 'hang-ups' these elders profess. Come to think of it, this was to some extent Jesus' way. He didn't produce one systematic, comprehensive statement of faith. His teaching was composed of numerous fragments, each of which point to some aspect of the truth. He was content to let his hearers put them together and discover wholeness for themselves.

The thing on which I believe there is wide agreement, is that all that is finest and best in our present society stems from the influence of Jesus. Our society has been formed and moulded by men and women seeking to follow his way in personal and social life. We are privileged to enjoy their legacy. It would be an absolute tragedy if our generation was to turn its back on the one who has given us so much and whose ways provide the only real hope for humankind.

CHANGE

I have to acknowledge that I have changed my views a number of times during my life! I was an ardent pacifist in my youth, but can no longer hold to that position. I was also a strong socialist believing in the public ownership of the means of production, distribution and exchange (Clause 4), but can no longer subscribe to that doctrine either - at least, not in the absolute way in which I once did. In church circles I once believed in the importance of maintaining strict orthodoxy; but I am now full of questions about various expressions of the faith.

In some cases my present view is a development of an earlier one, but in other cases it is diametrically opposed to it. Sometimes I now espouse a view which I once derided. This can be very depressing, and tempt you to give up and leave thinking to others of a more stable disposition.

Two things comfort me and encourage me to go on. Firstly, there is nothing worse than coming up against someone who has never changed his views and considers it a virtue to defend them to the death. And secondly, it is reassuring to find how many others who have given much to the world, have confessed to having had the same experience.

Arthur Koestler, one of the greatest brains of the 20th century, writes: 'Since my schooldays I have not ceased to marvel each year at the fool I had been the year before. Each year brought its own revelation and each time I could only think with shame and rage of the opinions I had held and vented before the last initiation. But lately the new revelations instead of shattering and destroying all that went before, seem to combine into a pattern sufficiently elastic to absorb the new material and yet with a certain consistency in its basic features.'

And Karl Jung, the psychiatrist, has said: 'All true things must change and only that which changes remains true'.

If we hold this view, however, we must recognise that the things that we now hold to be sacrosanct will also be subject to change. We're on a journey - individually and human kind as a whole - and we must be prepared for changing vistas and differing circumstances. George MacLeod says: 'If, as a community, we write at all, it can be no more than passing calculations in the sand, to point to the next obedience'.

Appreciating this, while not preventing us from stating our views strongly, should make us much more ready to listen to the sincere views of others and learn from them and to expect a fuller truth to be revealed to us. We must 'live by the light we have and pray for more light'. It is the 'next obedience' that matters, not the fading light of the past.

MYSTERY

In our search for truth and in our efforts to understand the nature of reality, we must always be prepared to acknowledge that certain things remain a mystery - and always will, given the limits of human understanding.

This is especially important for people who adopt a religious view of life. We must not be afraid to say: 'I honestly don't know'; 'I have no explanation'; 'It's a mystery to me'.

Paul says: 'Now we see through a glass darkly... Now I know (only) in part' (1 Cor. 13:12). And he also says (of the Deity): 'How unsearchable are His judgements and His ways past finding out' (Romans 11:33). Christianity does not come with answers to all the questions that fill the human mind.

Neither does Science. The fraud that some scientists perpetrate is that science has discovered (or more or less discovered, or is about to discover, or will discover) the explanation of all things and the answers to all questions. But although science has had remarkable successes in the physical field (i.e. the 'what' questions), it has nothing to say (as Science) about the 'why' questions (meaning and purpose, good and evil etc.).

Stephen Hawking in *A Brief History of Time* is honest about it. 'Up to now, most scientists have been too occupied with the development of new theories that describe *what* the universe is, to ask the question *why*'.

It is part of the human predicament that we have to live with this element of mystery in trying to make sense of the world and our place in it. It is no use pretending otherwise.

Arthur Koestler confesses: 'In my youth I regarded the universe as an open book, printed in the language of physical equations and social determinants: whereas now it appears to me as a text written in invisible ink, of which *in rare moments of grace,* we are able to decipher a small fragment' (emphasis author's).

We may ask: 'Why did God not make it all clear to us in the beginning?' That is part of the Mystery, to which we have to say 'I don't know'. But it does mean that instead of having our path in life all mapped out for us (which would be very boring), life is a continuing voyage of discovery in which we are rewarded with a feeling of achievement when we uncover a bit more of the truth.

In this life the mystery is never fully solved, but it is in working with the truth we have, that we gain the confidence and conviction which leads us on to a fuller and deeper understanding.

POETRY

'Poetry is the language of Religion', said the Scottish poet, George Bruce - a loyal elder of the Kirk. Maybe this isn't such good news for those of us who aren't much 'into' poetry - and I count myself in that category. But what he seems to be saying is that it's the poet's way of looking at life and describing it, that yields the deepest truths.

In this question, the rigid language of the Law - either moral or civil - is inadequate, even though morality is integral to a religious view of life. Similarly, the use of logic or reason - whether philosophical, theological or scientific - fails to express the full truth which underlies religion, though this is not to deny the importance of reason, or to suggest that religion is irrational.

Rather George Bruce is saying that it is the poetic vision which takes us closer to the heart of the truth we seek. It is the implements of the poet which we need to use - the poem and the parable, the metaphor and the myth, the story, the symbol, the imagery and the imagination. These are the vehicles which carry the truth which other words cannot express. And they not only inform; they touch our hearts and inspire us with a living truth for daily life. This is why the parables of Jesus are embedded in our culture and influence our lives today.

Have we therefore been too concerned to produce neat definitions and watertight statements of belief, which will enshrine the truth for all time, forgetting that the truth we seek 'passes man's understanding'? Rather it is in the groping, often partial, insights of the poet and the visionary (or prophet) that something of the veil is lifted and a deeper truth revealed.

In a similar vein, this way of thinking also applies to our use of the Bible. It was recently reported that a priest had said: 'Everything in the Bible is true, except the facts'! This is a gross exaggeration of course, and it's meant to shock and make us think. But it does remind us of the way we should use the Bible - not primarily as an accurate historical text or as a manual for scientific or evolutionary studies, but as a treasure chest of human experience in relation to God, from which we too may draw guidance and meaning for our own lives.

It should also release us from worries about whether all the facts recorded in the Bible can be squared with the results of modern scholarship and research. In this regard at least the Bible is not infallible. This is not to downgrade the Bible, but to direct us to the way in which we will find its richest treasures for our own lives. Paul Tillich talks about the 'inexhaustible meaning' of the great texts of the Bible. We should be content to savour this 'meaning' rather than expect strict literal 'truth' from every page of scripture.

OURSELVES

For some people today the question is not 'Does God exist?' but 'Do we exist?'

There is pressure on all sides to persuade us that there is nothing special about human beings. We're all just part of the material world about us - a concoction of substances producing chemical reactions to the world and to other people.

This is clearly a challenge to the widely-held presumption that we are distinct and unique beings. That we have a personality, a self, a soul, a spirit, which is of the essence of our nature. And that we are not adequately described merely in terms of our material characteristics.

To many, it will seem strange that, if we are all a collection of substances interacting with each other, one of these substances (the mind) is able to understand the real nature of the whole - including itself. It may also seem surprising that people who claim to believe in this materialistic view of human beings, still act as if there are 'real' persons involved in human intercourse. They describe people as 'good' or 'bad': they ascribe ulterior motives to people who disagree with them, and they are ready to argue heatedly with those who think differently from them.

One would have thought that such attitudes are excluded by a mechanistic view of human nature. If it's only chemical reactions that are taking place, then what's the point of arguing? You can't be held responsible for your chemical reactions! You're wasting your breath.

Clearly, ordinary human behaviour creates problems for people who hold this view. How do you account for courage, loyalty, honesty, goodness, unselfishness, sacrificial love etc? The simple materialistic explanation is not good enough.

Richard Dawkins, one of the proponents of the materialistic point of view, suggests that 'Perhaps the 'I' person that I feel myself to be is a kind of semi-illusion... The mind is a collection of fundamentally warring agents'. Does he really mean that a 'collection of warring agents' can prove that the 'I' which I feel myself to be is a semi-illusion?

Of course he prefaces that statement with the word 'perhaps' which means he has left the realm of scientific fact. It looks like guesswork - or worse, faith dressed up as science. The truth is that if you start out with a purely materialistic outlook, you will get only materialistic answers.

Christians can't prove that we exist as persons either. We do not understand how the soul relates to our physical make-up. But it is by accepting that reality, which seems to make sense in our daily life and experience, that we can begin to grow into our full stature as human beings.

RELIGION

I don't much like the word 'Religion'. It often just suggests something added on to your life - one factor among many. Worse still, it may refer to that which divides you from others - Catholic, Protestant, Muslim, Jew, Hindu etc. As such, it gives rise to unrealistic divisions which split communities and stand in the way of peace.

It's as well to remember that Jesus didn't come to set up a new religion. He wanted to talk about life - all life - and to help us to live more fully.

It's a pity, however, that 'religion' has such a bad name, as it does refer to something important. It is the effort of men and women in every age to express their belief about that area of their experience which is beyond the perception of their physical senses, but which impinges on their daily living. It is part of the age-long human effort to find meaning and purpose in life.

The fact that religion has such a negative image has led many people to turn their backs on it as a relic of mankind's primitive past and live as if the question which religion addresses doesn't matter. 'Forget all this religious stuff and get on with life', they say.

And yet... Many people, even among those without any formal religious convictions, would agree with Jesus that 'Man does not live by bread alone'. Indeed, one of the best-selling novels to come out of communist Russia was entitled 'Not By Bread Alone'. The purely materialistic view is widely recognised as inadequate. There is something more to human life than the continual acquisition and consumption of 'things'.

Maybe it is 'religion' as generally understood, that is getting in the way of people taking seriously the question it is meant to answer - especially if 'religious' people seem to have left the real world and spend their time arguing about obscure metaphysical ideas, which have little bearing on daily life.

Jesus was an ordinary human being and very much part of this world. But again and again he reminded his hearers of the extra dimension in human life which we dare not ignore. His aim was to awaken in us an awareness of those unseen spiritual forces which are part of the reality of life on earth.

John Baillie, the leading 20th Century Scottish theologian, captures the essence of this in one of his prayers:

> 'Let me not go forth today believing only in the world of sense and time.
> My life today will be lived in time, but eternal issues will be concerned in it.
> My business will be with things material, but behind them let me be aware of things spiritual.
> Let me keep steadily in mind that the things that matter are not money or possessions, but truth, honour and helpfulness'.

CREED

One of the concerns voiced by the Kirk Elder who led me to offer these 'fragments', was his difficulty in saying the Apostles' Creed with any 'honesty or conviction'. In this, I'm sure he's like many others. Phrases like 'He descended into Hell' or 'He ascended into Heaven' or 'He sitteth at the right hand of God the Father', are not consistent with what we know of the universe today. Even 'Conceived by the Holy Ghost, born of the Virgin Mary' or 'the Resurrection of the Body' require considerable re-interpretation to be maintained with any sort of honesty.

And yet this Creed is a great Statement of Belief which is meant to unite us and rally us to the cause of Christ. Too often it seems to leave us with feelings of guilt that we're not real Christians, and are really cheats for standing up and saying it.

It is important to remember that the Creeds and Confessions were often composed as a defiant statement of the Christian faith in a hostile world and that saints and martyrs found strength from them for their struggle against the forces which assailed them. In continuing to recite them, we are in some way declaring our unity with our forebears in that great tradition which gave so much to the world (and for which they often gave their lives).

But the creeds were composed in the context of the 'world-view' of those who wrote them. The early disciples were Jews and therefore their statements were full of references to Jewish imagery and tradition. The authors of the early creeds were concerned to bring together disparate Christian groups under one statement of belief, but it was inevitably in terms of their limited world-view. The Westminster Confession was composed at a time when the newly established Protestant Church needed a statement of its own position over against the Roman Catholic Church, and its references to the Pope and priests are unbelievably harsh by today's standards.

Such statements are always bound to reflect the world-view of the age in which they are written. They never can be 'final' or 'infallible'. And to make strict adherence to such statements a condition of joining the Christian community can often stifle the spirit of Christ which is always breaking out of human limitations and leading Christians to new ways of living.

I sometimes feel that it would be more meaningful to stand as a congregation and recite the Beatitudes or Isaiah 53 or 1 Corinthians 13 or the Prologue to St John's Gospel - or any of the other great biblical passages which would affirm and undergird our unity in the Spirit.

Despite all this, when I stand to recite the Creed with my fellow Christians, I try not to worry too much about the bits that don't make sense to me. I try to affirm as much as I can, knowing that in doing so I am joined in the spirit with those who in their day - and in their way - were loyal to the faith of Christ. It is a strong expression of the Communion of Saints.

GOD

Is belief in God any longer tenable in our modern world? Although no one seriously believes in the 'Old Man up in Heaven', such imagery still hangs around the word 'God' in popular use. We meet it (and sing about it) in hymns, old religious statements and indeed in parts of the Bible. And the public are quick to pin it on to church folk as an easy figure of fun and mockery. So why hold on to such a discredited term?

To lose the word 'God', and what it truly stands for, would be to lose something which has profoundly influenced the lives of men and women down the centuries. Karen Armstrong, an ex-nun, in her book *A History of God*, shows that in all lands and at all times, human beings have been engaged in a search for the origin and meaning of life, which they have identified with 'God'. And how they understood 'God' has played an important part in the personal and social development of us all. At least the idea of 'God' keeps us in our place and saves us from an exaggerated view of our own importance in the scheme of things.

Can we then form an idea of 'God' which will give meaning and purpose to our lives? If 'Poetry is the language of Religion' (George Bruce - see Fragment 3), we must be careful how we look for better definitions, which depend on mere words. Maybe the best we can do is to suggest one or two directions in which to look.

For instance John Baillie reminds us that God is the *'Uncreated One'*. That may not do much to help us identify God, but at least it reminds us that we are NOT talking about 'A' Being, but about *'BEING'* itself - beyond whom there is no Creator. When Moses asked: 'Who will I say has sent me?' he was told: 'Tell them 'I AM' has sent you'. God is the ground of all being.

A lot of our misunderstandings arise from our image of God as *static*, rather than as *dynamic*. A friend of mind told me recently: 'I think of God more and more as a Verb rather than as a Noun'. God is in the movement of life, in activity and Action. We need to look for God in what he is *doing*. And we find him by becoming involved in his work.

Basil of Caesarea, the Eastern Orthodox theologian says: 'We cannot see God intellectually. We know God only by his *operations*'. And he's not talking about spectacular, miraculous happenings. He sees God's 'operations' in the daily business of living. As John Baillie again said: 'We look for God nowhere else than in Goodness'. And when St John said: 'God is Love', he didn't just mean 'God is loving'. When we see Love or Goodness, there we see God.

But of course for the Christian, the Image of God is what they see in Jesus. The title 'Son of God' may be loaded with Jewish imagery and symbolism which doesn't do much for us. But St Paul says simply: '*God was in Christ*'. And it is in *Looking* at Jesus and *Listening* to Jesus and *Following* Jesus that we find God.

CHURCH

Unlike other religious leaders (Buddha, Confucius, Mohammed etc.) Jesus made no plans to set up an organisation to carry on his work after his death. His approach was almost breath-takingly casual for a man with such a momentous mission! The nearest he got to talking about the future was when he shared a special meal with his disciples just before his death and where he said that they were to think of the bread and wine as his body and blood - his presence with them. But he left no instructions as to how they were to organise their life together.

So it was as a MOVEMENT - a continuation of the campaign they had all been part of - that the world first met the Church. It was the emergence of pockets of Christian life in ever-increasing areas of the 'civilised world' which alarmed the authorities. They could have handled a religious institution and given it its place alongside the others. But the Christian Movement was like an organism working ceaselessly within the fabric of society and threatening to undermine the basis of its life with its new Christian values.

So today, wherever the Church is true to its origins it is present as a *movement in life rather than as an institution in society*. This is not to reject the existing Church of which we are part. Any movement as it grows requires organisation, and it is only through that organisation that it can co-ordinate and maximise its efforts. And of that huge organisation (the world-wide Church), we are all humble beneficiaries.

Institutions, however, can stifle organic movement. They need rules and regulations, codes and laws, and these can easily become the be-all and end-all of their existence. For some, the traditional Statements of Belief give strength to faith, and that it is good. For others, they are too rigid and limiting and can become stumbling-blocks. If we truly seek a 'Church Without Walls', then maybe one of the biggest walls to be removed is that of unchallengeable Dogma.

The truth is that any congregation includes members with widely different levels of faith. Some are glad to affirm the whole Bible, word for word, and the Creeds and Confessions too. Others just manage to cling on to the man Jesus and whatever else they can believe in. *But they are all followers of Jesus*, and *together* part of the Christian Movement. The Church was never meant to be an exclusive organisation. From the beginning it has been joyfully inclusive of 'all who love the Lord Jesus Christ'. We must make it clear; there is a place for all today.

If we are happy with the final paragraph of the introduction, I suggest that we need to:

1. Recognise that the Church is in a period of transition. The Church of the future will be different from the Church we know.

2. Affirm the Church today and associate ourselves with those parts of it where the movement is engaging with the world.

3. Make sure there is space for ALL 'Followers of Jesus'.

JESUS

A leading Czech Marxist philosopher, Machovec, wrote (in the '70s): 'Critics practically never reproach Christians for being followers of Christ, but for not being such; for betraying the name of Christ'. It is widely accepted in literature and in life, that Jesus is a universal criterion for goodness.

And yet Jesus slipped into the world and out again almost unobserved. He was a village carpenter for most of his life, with only a brief ministry of preaching and healing in Galilee and Judea about the year 30 AD. He was of little importance to contemporary society, and there is no record of his doings in the history of the day. He himself left no writings and we are dependent on the Gospels, written about 40 years later, for the scanty information we have about him. Even his death, which has meant so much to the world in subsequent centuries, was a small local event which merited no special mention in the chronicles of the Jews or the Romans.

Much of what Jesus taught can be found in the Old Testament and in other religions round about. But he went beyond the Old Testament. 'Love your enemies', 'Go the second mile', 'Return good for evil'. He challenged all Man's ideas about morality and justice, and proposed a new basis for human relationships.

And his life matched his teaching. You don't have to believe that Karl Marx lived an impeccable life to believe in Marxism. You don't have to admire Freud's personal life to be a Freudian. But the credibility of the Christian message depends on the character and life of Jesus; that his life matched his teaching.

Most unique however was Jesus' death. Other religious leaders - Moses, Mohammed, Buddha, and Confucius - all died in ripe old age, admired and respected, with clear instructions to their followers. Jesus died, a young man of thirty or so, expelled by 'decent' society, betrayed by his own disciples, forsaken by God and hanged on a Roman Cross. A 'total disaster' of a life!

And yet a few weeks later, we find his demoralised disciples out in the same streets again, proclaiming his Good News - Not in spite of his death, but precisely *because* of it. As he had said: 'Except a corn of wheat fall into the ground and die, it remains alone. But if it dies, it bears much fruit' (John 12:24). For the disciples, these stranger parts of his teaching were beginning to fall into place. *Somehow the Cross was not Defeat, but Victory.* The life of Jesus did not end on the Cross. 'Death could not hold him.' The power they had seen in Jesus was now liberated for the whole world. And they were privileged to be agents of it.

But how could they describe this unique person? From their Jewish background they came up with words like Messiah, Saviour, Son of God, and Redeemer. But we are not Jews and we may not feel so comfortable with such titles. May we not say however, that in Jesus, the life of God has been injected into the blood-stream of the world and continues to circulate with its life-giving power?

CROSS

The fact that a small group of Palestinian peasants captivated the Western world with their 'Good News', based on the life and teachings of a crucified criminal, is surely one of the great mysteries which historians must try to explain. The established gods of the Roman and Greek world did not lie down and give up. They were undermined and superseded by a faith that turned the world's values upside down and offered completely new values for the life of man. And the engine which powered the Christian mission across the Mediterranean world was the Cross of Jesus.

As well as being an instrument of extreme torture, a Roman cross was a mark of utter degradation, reserved for the worst criminals. To the Jews, it was the 'curse of God'. And yet instead of trying to hide this scandal, the disciples put it 'up front'. As Paul said: 'We preach Christ crucified, to the Jews a stumbling block, to the Greeks foolishness, but to us, the power of God and the wisdom of God'. (1 Cor. 1:23)

For these early disciples, the Cross encapsulated the whole life of Jesus, his compassion, his self-giving, his courage, his faithfulness unto death - all that they had known and admired during their brief time with him. Like everyone else, they accepted the evidence of their own eyes and believed that Jesus' death on the Cross was the end of their forlorn hopes and dreams. What changed their minds was the unforeseen, yet undeniable conviction that there was a spirit at work amongst them which they identified with their lost friend Jesus, convincing them that the Cross was not final defeat; that the ultimate victory does not lie with the powers of evil but with the forces of goodness and love.

So for Christians, the Cross is a reminder of that pivotal event in the life of the world. Christians don't subscribe to a Statement about the truth. They become involved in an Event - in a continuing event - at the heart of which is the cross of Jesus.

What overwhelmed the disciples was that in spite of their betrayal and desertion, Jesus had come back to them and called them into his service again. This was their forgiveness and release from guilt - to be allowed to be part of his life and mission again. And that's the way of our release too.

Paul says the Cross is the POWER of God. It is the power of the powerless; of a victim, not a conqueror. A shipyard manager who had been twice demoted (due to restructuring!) and found himself closer to the 'shop floor' than ever before, and used by the men for guidance and support, once said to me: 'Don't underestimate the strength of your weakness'.

Paul also said the Cross is the *wisdom* of God. Considering what we now know about the size and age of the universe, can we really claim that this small local event, 2000 years ago is of significance for all time? Only if we believe the Cross is the eternal Wisdom of God.

FAITH(S)

Firstly, FAITH. As the schoolboy said: 'Faith is believing what you know ain't true'. This, of course, confuses faith and belief; and although they overlap, they are different. Belief is more of an intellectual activity, whereas faith is 'an affair of the heart', expressed more in living than in words.

Everyone lives by faith. There are many uncertainties in life and we all have to develop some basis on which to make our choices. You can see people's choices by what is most important to them. Some put their faith in Pleasure, some in Power, some in Wealth, some in Indolence, some in Sex. It's the dominant factor in our lives which determines our lesser choices.

A Christian puts his faith in Jesus. We are Followers of Jesus. That's the faith that gives direction to our lives. Our faith is in a Person rather than in 'doctrines about a person'; this releases us from the straitjacket of 'definitions'. It liberates the human spirit and makes room for imagination, inspiration and new experience. But it is 'faith' not certainty. Mysteries and unresolved questions remain. As Archbishop Tutu said: 'Of course Faith is a risk - but one I would never risk living without'.

And another thing. Faith and Prayer are not far apart. When we engage in an act of goodness and love, and pray God's help in pursuing it, we may not always find it turns out the way we expect, but we will see the hand of God at work - frequently with a far better outcome.

Secondly, OTHER FAITHS. I cringe every time I hear a Church Leader referring to the church's membership (worthy though they be) as 'the people of God'. It suggests that other human beings are not 'God's People' and that somehow God will not be as interested in them as he is in us. Embedded in our thinking, of course, is a division of the world into Christian on the one hand and Heathen on the other. Without questioning the missionary zeal of the churches in bringing the Gospel to lands which have not heard of Christ, it does seem that there is a need today for greater dialogue and readiness to understand and rejoice in such truth as we find in other Faiths.

To discover truth in other religions is not to be disloyal to Christ. I believe he would approve. Jesus remains the Touchstone of Truth for Christians. But it is an exciting experience to find truth elsewhere. The Koran teaches: 'All truth comes from God and should be sought wherever it can be found'.

George Matheson, the blind minister who was one of the great hymn writers of the 19th Century, was ahead of his time when he wrote:

> Gather us in, Thou Love that fillest all,
> Gather our rival faiths within the fold
> Rend each man's temple-veil and bid it fall . . .
> Gather us in.

FOLLOWERS

When I was contemplating entering the Ministry in my late teens/early twenties, one question which made me hesitate, was whether I would be able to maintain my Faith throughout my life - and what would happen if I lost it.

In mulling this over I remember being not a little consoled by the thought that a life spent in trying to 'follow Jesus' and in encouraging others to do the same, could never be described as a 'wasted life'. There's a natural integrity about such a life, which is sufficient without support from any 'Statement of Belief'. At the time, I thought of this as a 'fall-back position' to save me from a feeling of failure and despair. Now I realise it is at the *core* of what it means to be a Christian.

Nor is it an easy option. It is the *hard* bit. But it's the only bit and that makes sense everywhere in the world and in every age. And it makes sense to both the greatest and the simplest of intellects. Christians are simply (and fully described as) 'Followers of Jesus'. If the God we seek is to be found in the life of Jesus, then we can't go wrong if we try to follow him. Martin Luther says: 'And here I let pass all curious speculations touching the divine majesty, and stay myself on the humanity of Christ'. And Jesus himself promises: 'They that do his will shall know the doctrine' (John 7:17) - not the other way round.

It seems to me that there's a difference between being called to join a group who are trying to follow Jesus in their lives and being asked to become a member of a Church. To become a Member is *'to join'*: to become a Follower is to *'join in'*! There may be wide variations amongst us in doctrinal belief or theological formulations, but the one thing that can give us unity, is a recognition of each other as co-followers of Jesus.

That means engaging with the world as he did; risking following a way of life which is at odds with the world's wisdom. Loving Enemies, Returning Good for Evil, Going the Extra Mile, Forgiving Seventy Times Seven, accepting the Role of the Servant and much more. It's a quite different way of dealing with the challenges of life, much more demanding, but much more rewarding - and many would say, much more effective.

On a recent T.V. programme an American Professor of Sociology was talking to a group of young people about telling the truth. 'But surely', he was challenged, 'honest people always come off worst in real life'. 'Yes', said the professor, 'if they play the same game as the cheats and liars. But they're really in a different ball-game. Theirs is about relationships, integrity and honour. That's where they win'.

For those who would follow Jesus, it's important to recognise the 'ball-game' we're in. If our real ball-game is about winning at all costs, getting things our way, keeping on top, then we'll always lose. But if our game is to bring everyone 'on-side', then in loving our enemies, we're on the only side that has any chance of ultimate victory.

Armstrong, Karen: *A History of God* (1994): Ballantine Books, New York

Baillie, John: *A Diary of Private Prayer* (1949): Charles Scribner's Sons, New York

Basil of Caesarea: *Works* (translated B Jackson) in *Nicene and Post-Nicene Fathers* 2nd Series vol 8 (1895); Edinburgh, T & T Clark

Bruce, George: personal conversation with author

Dawkins, Richard: *Unweaving the Rainbow* (1998): Penguin, London

Hawking: Stephen: *A Brief History of Time* (1988); Random, New York

Jung, Karl: *Memories, Dreams, Reflections* (1962): Routledge, London

Koestler, Arthur: *Arrow in the Blue* (1951): Macmillan, New York

Luther, Martin: Table Talk (various translations)

Machovec, Milan: *A Marxist Look at Jesus* (1976): Darton, Longman and Todd, London

MacLeod, George: 'The Inner Building', © Wild Goose Publications, from *Daily Readings With George MacLeod*, Wild Goose Publications, Glasgow G2 3DH www.ionabooks.com (Originally from the *Coracle*: the magazine of the Iona Community, 1965)

Tillich, Paul *Shaking the Foundations* (1955): Charles Scribner's Sons, New York

Tutu, Desmond: TV interview

ACKNOWLEDGEMENTS

Permission to reproduce 2 excerpts from Arrow in the Blue by Arthur Koestler sought from Macmillan Publishing Company (New York).

Excerpt from A Brief History of Time by Stephen W Hawking (1999) used by permission of Bantam, an imprint of Random House, Inc. (New York).

Excerpt from Unweaving the Rainbow: Science, Delusion and the Appetite for Wonder by Richard Dawkins (Allen Lane The Penguin Press, 1998), copyright © Richard Dawkins, 1998, reproduced by permission of Penguin Books Ltd.

Excerpts from A Diary of Private Prayer by John Baillie (1960) used by permission of Oxford University Press (Oxford).

Excerpt from A Marxist Look at Jesus by Milan Machovec (1976) used by permission of Darton, Longman & Todd Ltd. (London).

Permission to reproduce 'The Inner Building' by George MacLeod sought from Wild Goose Publications (Glasgow).